C000265429

THE LITTLE BOOK
OF
HYGGE
[HOO•GA]

JONNY JACKSON
& ELIAS LARSEN

THE LITTLE BOOK OF HYGGE

Summersdale Publishers Ltd
46 West Street
Chichester
West Sussex
PO19 1RP
UK

www.summersdale.com

Printed and bound in the Czech Republic

ISBN: 978-1-78685-207-6

Substantial discounts on bulk quantities of Summersdale books are available to corporations, professional associations and other organisations. For details contact general enquiries telephone: +44 (0) 1243 771107, fax: +44 (0) 1243 786300 or email: enquiries@summersdale.com.

summer sunshine on your cheeks and the grass between your toes – *hygge* is a state of being that can be enjoyed all year round.

This book will help you to kindle this Danish feeling of cosiness, peace and contentment in your own life. With a raft of simple tips and calming quotes, here you will find everything you need to make you feel truly *hyggelig* – full of *hygge*. Take a break, settle into your comfiest chair and celebrate the little things that make life good.

LIVE IN
ROOMS FULL
OF LIGHT.

Aulus Cornelius Celsus

LIGHT A CANDLE

Light a candle to fill your room with soft warmth. Whether you use a scented or unscented candle, and whether you light one candle or ten, the gently flickering light is the perfect way to evoke feelings of cosiness.

THIS MOMENT IS YOUR LIFE.

Omar Khayyám

It is the sweet, simple things of life which are the real ones after all.

Laura Ingalls Wilder

WATCH THE SUNRISE AND SUNSET

Whether you're an early bird or a night owl, there's always a chance to catch a breathtaking moment at the turn of the day. Wait in quiet reverie or enjoy the anticipatory excitement as you take time out of life's busy schedule and engage with nature and its simple beauty.

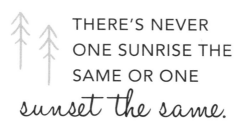

THERE'S NEVER
ONE SUNRISE THE
SAME OR ONE
sunset the same.

Carlos Santana

There is a serene and
settled majesty to
woodland scenery
that enters into the
soul and delights
and elevates it.

Washington Irving

GO FOR
WOODLAND
WALKS

Nothing beats a wrapped-up
walk on a chilly day. Make sure to
note the little things: the drops
of dew, the birds singing in the
trees, the crispy leaves under your
boots, the new buds in spring
or the blooming wildflowers.

The foolish man
seeks happiness in
the distance; the wise
grows it under his feet.

James Oppenheim

The snowdrop
and primrose our
woodlands adorn,
and violets bathe in
the wet o' the morn.

Robert Burns

WE NO LONGER
BUILD FIREPLACES
FOR PHYSICAL
WARMTH... WE BUILD
THEM TO DREAM
BY, TO HOPE BY,
TO HOME BY.

Edna Ferber

LIGHT A LOG FIRE

A simple fire can transform a plain room into somewhere cosy and inviting. The smoky smell, the warmth and the golden glow will draw you in and allow you to simply be. If you don't have a hearth, you could invest in a simple log-burning stove.

SMILE,
BREATHE
AND GO
SLOWLY.

Thích Nhất Hạnh

TRY A SIMPLE BREATHING EXERCISE

Begin by sitting or lying comfortably.
Place one hand on your stomach,
just below your ribcage.
Place the other over your chest.
Take a deep breath in through your
nose, taking care to inhale into your
abdomen. You should feel your hand
being pushed out by your stomach,
and your chest should stay stationary.
Hold for a moment before breathing
out slowly through pursed lips
until you can't exhale any more.
You should begin to feel relaxed after
two or three cycles of this exercise, but
continue for as long as you need to.

ADOPT THE PACE OF NATURE: HER SECRET IS PATIENCE.

Ralph Waldo Emerson

THERE IS NO
DOUBT THAT
CREATIVITY
IS THE MOST
IMPORTANT
HUMAN
RESOURCE
OF ALL.

Edward de Bono

He is happiest, be he
king or peasant, who
finds peace in his home.

Johann Wolfgang von Goethe

MAKE YOURSELF COMFORTABLE

Sometimes something as simple as slipping on a pair of thick, fluffy socks can bring you comfort. Round off the cold edges and keep yourself cosy; it's often the little things that make a big difference.

BE HAPPY WITH
WHAT YOU HAVE
AND ARE, BE
GENEROUS WITH
BOTH, AND YOU
WON'T HAVE
TO HUNT FOR
HAPPINESS.

William Ewart Gladstone

LISTEN

From jazz music to classical, the sound of the crackling fire to the patter of rain on a conservatory roof – you know the sounds that connect with you, force you to slow down and make you daydream. Let sound relax your mind.

MUSIC EXPRESSES
THAT WHICH
CANNOT BE PUT
INTO WORDS.

Victor Hugo

IMAGINATION
IS THE
HIGHEST
KITE ONE
CAN FLY.

Lauren Bacall

NATURE DOES
NOT HURRY, YET
EVERYTHING IS
accomplished.

Lao Tzu

TAKE A BATH

Sink into a bath of steam, bubbles and scents to lighten your mood and relax your mind. Feel the bliss – and don't forget the salts, oils and a fluffy towel to envelop you when you're done.

I have just three things
to teach: simplicity,
patience, compassion.
These three are your
greatest treasures.

Lao Tzu

GO ON
A PICNIC

Whether with friends or on your own, a picnic is a wonderful way to reconnect with nature. Pack a few items of food and drink, take time to stroll to a quiet spot and enjoy the fresh air and greenery around you.

There are few
things so pleasant
as a picnic eaten in
perfect comfort.

W. Somerset Maugham

WHAT IS THE GOOD
OF YOUR STARS
AND TREES, YOUR
SUNRISE AND THE
WIND, IF THEY DO
NOT ENTER INTO
OUR DAILY LIVES?

E. M. Forster

I GO TO NATURE TO
BE SOOTHED AND
HEALED, AND TO
HAVE MY SENSES
PUT IN ORDER.

John Burroughs

MAKE TIME FOR TOGETHERNESS

Make time away from work and screens to connect with your loved ones. Try a board game or play charades – appreciate their laughter, conversation and company, and simply enjoy time together.

LIFE IS MORE
FUN IF YOU
PLAY GAMES.

Roald Dahl

JUST LIVING IS
NOT ENOUGH...
ONE MUST HAVE
SUNSHINE,
FREEDOM, AND
A LITTLE FLOWER.

Hans Christian Andersen

Dream as if you'll
live forever. Live as
if you'll die today.

James Dean

HOT CHOCOLATE

Treat yourself to a home-made hot chocolate. Warm the milk, cocoa powder and sugar, and maybe even add cinnamon, whipped cream and marshmallows. This classic drink is the perfect way to make you feel cosy from the inside out.

WARM TEA,
GOOD BOOKS,
SOFT PILLOWS,
FINE COMPANY.

Anonymous

Do not anticipate trouble,
or worry about what
may never happen.
Keep in the sunlight.

Benjamin Franklin

NOW AND THEN IT'S GOOD TO PAUSE IN OUR PURSUIT OF HAPPINESS AND JUST BE HAPPY.

Guillaume Apollinaire

CHOCOLATE FONDUE

A chocolate fondue is an easy
way to bring a little decadence
to an evening in with friends.
Slice some fruit, melt a large bar
of chocolate, and revel in the sweet
luxury of this heavenly treat.

THERE'S
NOTHING
BETTER THAN
A GOOD FRIEND,
EXCEPT A GOOD
FRIEND WITH
CHOCOLATE.

Linda Grayson

WITH FREEDOM,
BOOKS, FLOWERS
AND THE MOON,
WHO COULD NOT
BE HAPPY?

Oscar Wilde

READ

Settle onto the sofa with a good
book and enjoy being drawn
into a story, and away from the
rush of daily life. Reading can
be the perfect way to unwind
or escape for a moment whilst
still enriching your mind.

NO
ENTERTAINMENT
IS SO CHEAP AS
READING, NOR
ANY PLEASURE
so lasting.

Mary Wortley Montagu

IF YOU HAVE
A GARDEN AND
A LIBRARY,
YOU HAVE
EVERYTHING
YOU NEED.

Marcus Tullius Cicero

THE ORDINARY ACTS
WE PRACTISE EVERY
DAY AT HOME ARE OF
MORE IMPORTANCE
TO THE SOUL THAN
THEIR SIMPLICITY
MIGHT SUGGEST.

Thomas Moore

ATTITUDE IS A
LITTLE THING
THAT MAKES A
big difference.

Winston Churchill

What on earth could
be more luxurious
than a sofa, a book
and a cup of coffee?

Anthony Trollope

PRACTISE YOGA

Reconnect with your body and try out some yoga. Find a quiet space and a few minutes in your day and relish the feeling of gently stretching your body and your muscles. Even just ten minutes of yoga a day can help to clear your mind and bring you a sense of peace.

Yoga is a way to
freedom. By its
constant practice,
we can free ourselves
from fear, anguish
and loneliness.

Indra Devi

A CONTENTED MIND
IS THE GREATEST
BLESSING A MAN
CAN ENJOY IN
THIS WORLD.

Joseph Addison

STRETCH
YOUR LEGS

Running can be a way to both
settle the mind and invigorate your
senses. Whether you run around
town or out in the countryside, revel
in the feeling of freedom that it
brings, and enjoy coming back to
the warmth of your home, feeling
the rosy glow on your cheeks.

RUNNING IS A THING WORTH DOING... BECAUSE OF HOW IT FEEDS OUR BODIES AND MINDS AND SOULS IN THE PRESENT.

Kevin Nelson

Keep fresh flowers
in the home for their
beauty, fragrance,
and the lift they
give our spirits.

Andrew Weil

BRING THE OUTSIDE IN

A simple bunch of daffodils or a freshly cut branch of foliage is the easiest way of adding a natural touch to your home. Whether you go for the heady scent of roses or the delicate perfume of wild flowers such blooms bring a breath of fresh air from outside in.

I'D RATHER HAVE
ROSES ON MY
TABLE THAN
DIAMONDS ON
MY NECK.

Emma Goldman

Wherever you go,
no matter what the
weather, always bring
your own sunshine.

Anthony J. D'Angelo

HOW COULD
SUCH SWEET AND
WHOLESOME HOURS
BE RECKONED
BUT WITH HERBS
AND FLOWERS?

Andrew Marvell

CULTIVATE
HOUSE
PLANTS

If you would rather bring nature indoors more permanently, house plants are a wonderful way to brighten up a room as they last longer than a bunch of flowers. Their life and colour will lift your spirits and bring the calm of the natural world to your home.

MAY THE
COUNTRYSIDE
AND THE GLIDING
VALLEY STREAMS
CONTENT ME.

Virgil

WHAT IS
PARADISE?
BUT A GARDEN,
AN ORCHARD
OF TREES
AND HERBS,
FULL OF ALL
PLEASURE,
AND NOTHING
THERE BUT
DELIGHTS.

William Lawson

HERBS ARE THE
FRIEND OF THE
PHYSICIAN AND
THE PRIDE
of cooks.

Charlemagne

GROW A HERB GARDEN

There's nothing more rewarding than eating something you've grown yourself, and a herb garden is a simple way to grow-your-own. Fresh herbs are low-maintenance and can fit easily on a windowsill, but can make a real difference to your food.

GREEN FINGERS ARE
THE EXTENSION OF
A VERDANT HEART.

Russell Page

Nothing compares to
the simple pleasure
of a bike ride.

John F. Kennedy

GO ON A
BIKE RIDE

Reinvigorate your body and mind
with a bike ride. Feel the sun on
your face and the wind in your
hair, and revel in the freedom
that two wheels can give you.

WHEN THE STOMACH IS FULL, THE HEART IS GLAD.

Dutch proverb

HAPPINESS
IS
HOME-MADE.

Anonymous

I BELIEVE THAT
A SIMPLE AND
UNASSUMING
MANNER OF LIFE
IS BEST FOR
EVERYONE, BEST
FOR BOTH THE BODY
AND THE MIND.

Albert Einstein

Live in each season
as it passes: breathe
the air, drink the
drink, taste the fruit.

Henry David Thoreau

GO FRUIT PICKING

Fruit picking is a great way to spend an afternoon with family and friends. Search the hedgerows for blackberries or elderberries, or find a farm that invites you to pick fruit. Savour the sharp sweetness of raspberries or strawberries as you pick them, but remember to also take some home to make a delicious dessert.

TASTE EVERY FRUIT
OF EVERY TREE
IN THE GARDEN
AT LEAST ONCE.
IT IS AN INSULT
TO CREATION NOT
TO EXPERIENCE
IT FULLY.

Stephen Fry

KEEP SMILING,
BECAUSE LIFE
IS A BEAUTIFUL
THING AND
THERE'S SO
MUCH TO
SMILE ABOUT.

Marilyn Monroe

DON'T HURRY,
DON'T WORRY. AND
BE SURE TO SMELL
THE FLOWERS
ALONG THE WAY.

Walter Hagen

TAKE IT SLOW

Take the time to go slowly.
When life feels rushed and busy,
don't be afraid to turn down an
invite, or to say no. Make time
and space for yourself to stop
and recharge your batteries.

There is more to
life than increasing
its speed.

Mahatma Gandhi

Have nothing in your houses that you do not know to be useful, or believe to be beautiful.

William Morris

DECLUTTER

Try decluttering to bring some
order to your environment and
a sense of calm to your mind.
You don't have to overturn your
whole house to do this. Even just
tidying one drawer or one corner
of a room can fill you with a sense
of satisfaction and contentment.

WE NEED
MUCH LESS
THAN WE
THINK WE
NEED.

Maya Angelou

When you declutter...
it is astounding
what will flow into
that space that will
enrich you, your life
and your family.

Peter Walsh

I LINGERED MOST
ABOUT THE
FIREPLACE, AS THE
MOST VITAL PART
OF THE HOUSE.

Henry David Thoreau

STACK AND STORE FIREWOOD

There is a strange beauty in organised firewood, and it's easy to achieve. Make sure to cut the logs down to small lengths and store in a dry, well-ventilated store – this way the logs will be dry and ready to heat up your home whenever the mood takes you.

HE WHO IS
CONTENTED
IS RICH.

Lao Tzu

THE SIGHT OF THE
STARS ALWAYS
makes me dream.

Vincent Van Gogh

GO
STARGAZING

Find that tranquil feeling by looking
out at the night sky. Enjoy the
moment with friends or just sit by
yourself wondering at the scope
of the Milky Way, or simply watch
the stars twinkling above you.

Sitting back in the evening, stargazing and stroking your dog, is an infallible remedy.

Ralph Waldo Emerson

There is no feeling
more comforting
and consoling than
knowing you are
right next to the
one you love.

Anonymous

TOAST MARSHMALLOWS

Bring your family and friends together around a campfire and make an evening to remember by toasting marshmallows. Let go and delight your inner child with this messy, sticky but delicious treat.

COLLECT MOMENTS, NOT THINGS.

Anonymous

HOME IS THE
NICEST WORD
THERE IS.

Laura Ingalls Wilder

BE NOT AFRAID OF
GOING SLOWLY, BE
AFRAID ONLY OF
standing still.

Chinese proverb

PLAY CARDS

Switch off your screens and pick up some cards instead, and introduce some good-natured competition to your cosy gathering. However many players you have, there are plenty of games to keep you entertained for hours.

TIME
YOU ENJOY
WASTING IS
NOT WASTED
TIME.

Marthe Troly-Curtin

MAY YOUR WALLS
KNOW JOY; MAY
EVERY ROOM HOLD
LAUGHTER AND
EVERY WINDOW
OPEN TO GREAT
POSSIBILITY.

Mary Anne Radmacher

In the dew of little
things the heart
finds its morning
and is refreshed.

Kahlil Gibran

WATCH
A MOVIE

Whether it's a favourite from your teenage years, a romance that brings you warmth or a film with the feel-good factor, watching a movie in the comfort of your home is a wonderful way to switch off and unwind for an evening.

HOW BEAUTIFUL IT IS TO BE ALIVE!

Henry S. Sutton

To be with old friends
is very warming
and comforting.

Anonymous

SHARE FOOD TOGETHER

Sharing food together is a simple way to kindle a sense of community with the people around you. Whether it's a short lunch with colleagues or a longer evening with family and friends, enjoy the feeling of kinship as you share time together over food.

ONE CANNOT THINK
WELL, LOVE WELL,
SLEEP WELL,
IF ONE HAS NOT
DINED WELL.

Virginia Woolf

It is in his pleasures
that a man really lives;
it is from his leisure
that he constructs the
true fabric of self.

Agnes Repplier

WEAR COSY CLOTHES

Pulling on your favourite oversized jumper or snuggling under a large blanket is the best way to evoke the *hyggelig* feeling of comfort and cosiness.

EATING TOGETHER IS
THE MOST INTIMATE
FORM OF KINSHIP.

Natalie Jeremijenko

NOT JUST THE
PASSING OF
TIME. LIFE IS THE
COLLECTION OF
EXPERIENCES.

Jim Rohn

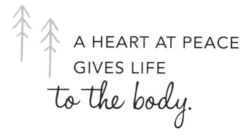

A HEART AT PEACE
GIVES LIFE
to the body.

Proverbs 14:30

PUT PEN
TO PAPER

Rekindle old friendships or reach
out to your loved ones by writing
a short letter or a postcard.
Taking the time to put pen to
paper, and to think about the
relationships you appreciate in
your life, is a wonderful way to lift
your spirits and feel connected.

THERE IS NO
GREATNESS WHERE
THERE IS NOT
SIMPLICITY.

Leo Tolstoy

A FRIEND
IS ONE OF
THE NICEST
THINGS YOU
CAN HAVE,
AND ONE OF
THE BEST
THINGS YOU
CAN BE.

Douglas Pagels

Find something you're passionate about and keep tremendously interested in it.

Julia Child

USE TEXTURE

Use texture to create a *hyggelig* feeling in your home. Chunky knitted furnishings, woollen rugs, sheepskin cushions and wooden elements bring with them a comfortable yet grounded atmosphere.

Your home should tell your story. What you love most collected and assembled in one place.

Nate Berkus

He enjoys true
leisure who has
time to improve
his soul's estate.

Henry David Thoreau

THERE IS NOTHING
LIKE STAYING AT
HOME, FOR
real comfort.

Jane Austen

RELAX IN LOUNGEWEAR

Being comfortable in your clothes
goes a long way to helping
you relax. Whether you prefer
pyjamas, loungewear, jeans or
jumpers, make yourself feel relaxed
in your own skin with clothes
that make you feel at ease.

A HOUSE THAT
DOES NOT
HAVE ONE
WARM, COMFY
CHAIR IN IT
IS SOULLESS.

May Sarton

TREAT YOURSELF TO SOMETHING SWEET

Treat yourself to something sweet to brighten your day mid-week. Raisin swirls, custard turnovers, cinnamon rolls, strawberry pinwheels – freshly baked or reheated, pastries can provide a delicious and homely comfort.

Wake up every morning
with the thought that
something wonderful
is going to happen.

Anonymous

LIFE IS MADE UP...
OF LITTLE THINGS,
IN WHICH SMILES
AND KINDNESSES
AND SMALL
OBLIGATIONS,
GIVEN HABITUALLY,
ARE WHAT WIN
AND PRESERVE
THE HEART.

Humphry Davy

MAKE A
MOOD BOARD

Make a mood board of things that
relax and inspire you: the colours
from the world around you; the
smile of a loved one; the swirl
of steam over a cup of coffee.
A visual reminder of appreciating
the little things that make life
good can be a real tonic.

The true secret of
happiness lies in
taking a genuine
interest in all the
details of daily life.

William Morris

Since time is the one immaterial object which we cannot influence...
it is an imponderably valuable gift.

Maya Angelou

THERE IS
REALLY NO
SUCH THING AS
BAD WEATHER,
ONLY DIFFERENT
KINDS OF GOOD
WEATHER.

John Ruskin

APPRECIATE THE WEATHER

Take time to appreciate all kinds of weather: the pattern of raindrops, the rich smell of damp earth and the wild power of the wind. There's beauty to be found everywhere, in a thunderstorm as well as in the sunshine.

SOME OLD-
FASHIONED THINGS
LIKE FRESH AIR
AND SUNSHINE ARE
HARD TO BEAT.

Laura Ingalls Wilder

A RAINY DAY IS
THE PERFECT TIME
FOR A WALK IN
the woods.

Rachel Carson

LIE ON YOUR
BACK AND
LOOK AT
THE STARS.

H. Jackson Brown Jr

GO FISHING

Try your hand at fishing and find
tranquillity by the side of a lake
or river. Enjoy the quiet on your
own or with a friend, and give
yourself time to think amongst
the beauty of the natural world.

THERE IS
CERTAINLY
SOMETHING
IN ANGLING
THAT TENDS
TO PRODUCE
A SERENITY
OF THE MIND.

Washington Irving

TRY BAKING

Your house is never more homely than when it's filled with the aroma of freshly baked bread, cake or biscuits. Baking can be therapeutic in itself, but sharing your creations with family and friends is an extra reward.

If baking is any
labour at all, it's a
labour of love.

Regina Brett

ENJOY THE LITTLE
THINGS, FOR ONE
DAY YOU MAY LOOK
BACK AND REALISE
THEY WERE THE
BIG THINGS.

Robert Brault

BURN ESSENTIAL OILS

Burning essential oils and focusing on their scents can be a calming and soothing experience.
With lavender or camomile for relaxation, rose and citrus to pep you up and pine or tea tree to cleanse there are countless oils to choose from to suit any occasion.

NOTHING IS WORTH MORE THAN THIS DAY.

Johann Wolfgang von Goethe

ASK YOURSELF
WHAT MAKES YOU
come alive.

Howard Thurman

SWITCH OFF
YOUR TECH

Switch off your screens and spend
an evening without your phone,
tablet or laptop. By disconnecting
with technology you can reconnect
with yourself, and make time
for you and your thoughts.

ALONE
IS
STRONG.

Swedish proverb

Technology...
interrupts our ability
to have a thought or a
daydream, to imagine
something wonderful.

Steven Spielberg

Contentment is
natural wealth.

Socrates

A peaceful mind
generates power.

Norman Vincent Peale

DOST THOU
LOVE LIFE?
THEN DO NOT
SQUANDER TIME,
FOR THAT IS
THE STUFF LIFE
IS MADE OF.

Benjamin Franklin

WRITE
A JOURNAL

The act of writing is therapeutic, and a great way to bring you peace of mind. Record your thoughts, feelings or worries, or simply recount moments from your day, and enjoy a few minutes of quiet reflection.

People who keep journals
have life twice.

Jessamyn West

COOKING IS LIKE
LOVE. IT SHOULD
BE ENTERED INTO
WITH ABANDON
OR NOT AT ALL.

Harriet Van Horne

COOK FROM SCRATCH

Cooking a dish from scratch is incredibly rewarding, and a wonderful way to bond with family and friends. Enjoy the challenge, whether your meal is successful or not, and appreciate the time spent together with your loved ones.

COOKING AND BAKING IS BOTH PHYSICAL AND MENTAL THERAPY.

Mary Berry

The purpose of life is to live it... to reach out eagerly and without fear for newer and richer experience.

Eleanor Roosevelt

Crafts make us feel
rooted, give us a
sense of belonging
and connect us
with our history.

Phyllis George

CRAFTS

Creating a handmade gift will fill
you with a sense of achievement,
and recipients of your efforts will
love the character and originality
they display. Try knitting, card
making or painting to give
your gifts a *hyggelig* touch.

I'm going to make
everything around
me beautiful – that
will be my life.

Elsie de Wolfe

LOOK DEEP INTO
NATURE, AND
THEN YOU WILL
UNDERSTAND
EVERYTHING BETTER.

Albert Einstein

GO CAMPING

Enjoy time away from routine
and immerse yourself in the great
outdoors by going camping.
Sleep on the ground, cook
amongst wildlife and wake up
to birdsong in the trees above.
Nothing is more life-affirming
than being so close to nature.

THE STARS ARE THE STREET LIGHTS OF ETERNITY.

Anonymous

IF MORE OF
US VALUED
FOOD AND
CHEER AND
SONG ABOVE
HOARDED
GOLD, IT
WOULD BE
A MERRIER
WORLD.

J. R. R. Tolkien

Burn the candles, use the nice sheets, wear the fancy lingerie. Don't save it for a special occasion. Today is special.

Regina Brett

LET US BE
GRATEFUL TO
PEOPLE WHO
make us happy.

Marcel Proust

FEAR LESS, HOPE
MORE... TALK LESS,
SAY MORE; HATE
LESS, LOVE MORE;
AND ALL GOOD
THINGS ARE YOURS.

Swedish proverb

If you're interested in finding out more about our books, find us on Facebook at **Summersdale Publishers** and follow us on Twitter at **@Summersdale**.

www.summersdale.com